CUBE
BOOK

CUBE BOOK

DOGS

WHITE STAR PUBLISHERS

TESTS BY

VITO BUONO

**project manager
and editorial director**
VALERIA MANFERTO DE FABIANIS

editorial coordination
GIADA FRANCIA

graphic design
CLARA ZANOTTI

translation
SARAH PONTING

© 2006 WHITE STAR S.P.A.
VIA CANDIDO SASSONE, 22-24
13100 VERCELLI - ITALY
WWW.WHITESTAR.IT

• A goose tolerates the curiosity of a German Shepherd puppy.

ISBN 88-544-0110-2

REPRINTS:
1 2 3 4 5 6 10 09 08 07 06

Printed in China
Color separation: CTM, Turin - Grafotitoli, Milan

CONTENTS

DOGS

INTRODUCTION   page   14

BREEDS AND PORTRAITS   page   28

IRRESISTIBLE MADCAPS   page 266

FOUR-LEGGED DREAMS   page 426

WILD RELATIVES   page 490

DOGS, CATS & CO.   page 550

LIFELONG COMPANIONS   page 592

HABITS AND BEHAVIOR   page 648

BIOGRAPHY, INDEX
REFERENCES   page 728

1 • A young Basset Hound watches with curious eyes.

2-3 • A Bearded Collie "flies" through the meadows.

4-5 • Living together is simply a matter of habit for dogs and cats.

6-7 • A mountain of wrinkles almost completely hides the face of a Chinese Shar-Pei.

10-11 • Two Labrador Retrievers sleep the deep slumber of puppies.

12-13 • The Basset Hound is a sociable and patient dog.

Introduction

"WE HAVE HAD CIVILIZATIONS WITHOUT HORSES AND EVEN CIVILIZATIONS WITHOUT THE WHEEL, BUT NEVER CIVILIZATIONS WITHOUT DOGS. NO DOGS, NO HUMANITY." PIERO SCANZIANI'S WORDS, SET DOWN IN HIS BOOK ENTITLED *IL CANE UTILE* (THE USEFUL DOG), PUBLISHED BY PAN, ROME, HAVE A DEEP EFFECT ON THE READER, FOR IF WE STOP TO THINK, THEY ARE NEITHER AN ATTENTION-GRABBING PHRASE NOR A PARADOX, BUT THE PURE TRUTH, BACKED UP BY SCIENCE. INDEED, IF THE MAXIM "NO DOGS, NO HUMANITY" WERE NOT TRUE, WE WOULD HAVE TO ASK OURSELVES WHY MAN HAS KEPT DOGS IN ALL PLACES AND AT ALL TIMES – AND NOT JUST FOR 14,000 OR 15,000 YEARS, AS WAS BELIEVED UNTIL A SHORT TIME AGO, BUT FOR AL-

• The mother Dalmatian has her work cut out with her pups, which can number up to 15 per litter!

Introduction

MOST 100,000 AS RECENT STUDIES ON THE MITOCHON-
DRIAL DNA OF OUR FOUR-LEGGED COMPANIONS HAVE RE-
VEALED. IF MAN HAS SHARED HIS LIFE AND HIS VERY EVO-
LUTIONARY HISTORY WITH THIS ANIMAL CONTINUOUSLY,
THEN THERE MUST BE A REASON FOR IT, AND THIS REASON
MUST UNDOUBTEDLY BE FOUND IN THE DOG'S EXTRAORDI-
NARY CAPACITY TO INTERACT WITH THE LIFE OF HUMANS
IN SUCH AN INCISIVE MANNER AS TO HAVE MADE IT ESSEN-
TIAL FOR MAN'S VERY SURVIVAL. PRIMITIVE PEOPLES SOON
DISCOVERED THIS WHEN THEY REALIZED THAT THEY CO-
ULD SLEEP EASIER IF THEIR CAVES OR CAMPS WERE GUAR-
DED BY DOGS, AND EAT MORE AND BETTER IF THEY COULD
HUNT WITH THE AID OF THE DOGS' SENSES OF SMELL AND
HEARING. LATER ON, WHEN THEY CHANGED FROM A NO-
MADIC TO A SETTLED LIFESTYLE, RAISING ANIMALS INSTEAD

Introduction

OF HUNTING THEM AND FARMING THE LAND RATHER THAN RELYING ON THE UNCERTAIN QUEST FOR WILD FRUIT AND ROOTS, THEY DISCOVERED THAT DOGS COULD HELP THEM TO DEFEND THEIR HERDS FROM PREDATORS AND THEIR TERRITORY FROM INVADERS. AFTER MAN HAD SATISFIED HIS PRIMARY NEEDS, HE BECAME A CONQUEROR AND EX-PLORER AND DOGS BECAME EXCELLENT SOLDIERS AND, LATER, AGILE AND UNTIRING CARRIERS AND EVEN ASTRO-NAUTS. HOWEVER, THAT IS NOT THE END OF THE STORY. EVEN AFTER MAN HAD LEFT THE STAGE OF PRIMARY NEEDS BEHIND, HE DID NOT FORGET ABOUT DOGS; AS HE GRADUALLY REFINED HIS LIFESTYLE AND CIVILIZATION, HE ALSO REFINED THE APPEARANCE AND EVEN SKILLS OF HIS FAITHFUL COMPANIONS, BY BREEDING THEM FOR ENHAN-CING DESIRED TRAITS. ALMOST 400 RECOGNIZED BREEDS

Introduction

EXIST TODAY AND CREATE AN ARMY OF SPECIALISTS FOR ALL OF MAN'S NEEDS – NO LONGER JUST FOR HUNTING AND DEFENSE. WE NOW RECOGNIZE THAT MAN HAS LEFT A DECISIVE MARK ON THE EVOLUTIONARY HISTORY OF DOGS, BUT IT WOULD NOT BE TOO FAR-FETCHED TO SAY THAT DOGS HAVE IN TURN INFLUENCED THE EVOLUTIONARY HISTORY OF MAN, ALBEIT NOT SO PROFOUNDLY. IN SHORT, THE TWO SPECIES ARE SO CLOSELY INTEGRATED AS TO SUGGEST A SINGLE COEVOLUTIONARY PROCESS, RATHER THAN TWO DISTINCT ONES.

19 • Although the Bulldog's massive head and expression are an awe-inspiring sight, this breed is extremely friendly by nature.

20-21 • Dogs express their contentedness by licking.

22-23 and 24-25 • The excitement of racing seems to trigger ancestral instincts of hunting, competition and socialization.

26-27 • Chow Chows were once proud hunters, and their thick coat gives them a haughty appearance.

BREEDS AND PORTRAITS

The Boxer is a sturdy and well-balanced dog, as demonstrated by this fine specimen.

INTRODUCTION Breeds and Portraits

It is possible to read not only a dog's story, but also its character and personality in its face. While it is true that each breed has a story to tell, it is also true that each individual dog has its own personal tale to recount, which makes it a unique and unrepeatable being, different from all others. You need only let yourself be guided by the feelings conveyed by looking at a dog in order to understand the concept. It is the same as with portraits: the clothes, eyes, posture, good looks or frailty of a body suffice to tell us who the person is, where he or she comes from and whom he or she has frequented. There are those with wrinkled faces, like great old men who have understood

INTRODUCTION Breeds and Portraits

THE MEANING OF A LIFE SPENT FIGHTING TO THE LAST, OR VETERAN WARRIORS WHO HAVE SURVIVED THE DANGERS OF WAR. THERE ARE THOSE WITH A PROUD STANCE, FEARLESS AND RUSTIC RANGERS WHO HAVE NOT YIELDED TO SHREWD BANDITS OR CUNNING PREDATORS. THERE ARE THOSE WHO DISPLAY A NATURAL REGALITY, WHOSE PROUD DEPORTMENT AND MANNERS CAN ONLY HAVE BEEN ACQUIRED BY FREQUENTING PRINCES AND KINGS. THE SHEPHERDS' AND FARMERS' DOGS, ON THE OTHER HAND, ARE RECOGNIZABLE BY THEIR HUMBLER, PROTECTIVE LOOKS, WITHOUT ANY FRILLS, AND THE BUSY AIR OF THOSE WHO KNOWN THAT THERE IS NO TIME FOR TRIFLES WHEN THE FLOCKS, BARNYARD, FARM AND HARVESTS NEED TO BE GUARDED. THE PORTRAIT OF THE PAMPERED LITTLE LAP-

Breeds and Portraits

DOG THAT HAS TO LOOK AFTER THE HOUSEHOLD MOOD IS COMPLETELY DIFFERENT. ITS EYES – WHETHER HIDDEN UNDER A FRINGE OR NOT – ARE LIKE THOSE OF A MOVIE DIRECTOR, PAYING ATTENTION TO ALL ASPECTS OF THE FILM OF DOMESTIC LIFE. EVEN THE ANONYMOUS FACE OF THE MONGREL, IF YOU LOOK AT IT WITH FEELING, WILL CONVEY A STORY OF HARDSHIPS OR RECOUNT A DESTINY THAT HAS NOT BEEN ABLE TO COUNT ON THE PRIVILEGES OF BLUE BLOOD, BUT WILL ALWAYS SPEAK OF A DEVOTION THAT IS UTTERLY DEVOID OF REVENGE OR GRUDGES. INDEED, IT WILL OFTEN HAVE THOSE WELL-WORN AND ARTFUL LOOKS THAT FORM ON THE FACES OF THOSE WHO HAVE HAD TO FEND FOR THEMSELVES.

* The Poodle is a perfect apartment dog and is able to sport the most bizarre "hairstyles."

Komondor

34 ● The shaggy Komondor is a determined, intuitive shepherd dog.

34-35 ● The matted hair of the Komondor makes this breed exempt from the usual grooming routines.

German Shepherd

36 • The versatile German Shepherd is the quintessential working dog and is employed in numerous fields, from lifesaving and guiding the blind to drug detection.

37 • The German Shepherd's attentive expression emphasizes one of its most sought-after traits: its ceaseless vigilance.

Well-developed and
well-proportioned
muscles give the
German Shepherd's
gait a powerful
elegance.

Belgian Sheepdog

40 • "Ready for action" - the attentive expression of the Belgian Sheepdog is one of the breed's main characteristics.

40-41 • Two Belgian Sheepdogs survey their surroundings, their necks carried proudly and their bodies poised.

Shetland Sheepdog
(Sheltie)

42 • The Shetland Sheepdog, or Sheltie, has a very noble appearance, with elegant proportions and a long, soft coat.

43 • A thick white "mane" sets off this Sheltie's narrow and intelligent face. This breed is very similar to the Rough Collie, but smaller.

Pembroke Welsh Corgi

- The low-set Pembroke Welsh Corgi, just 10-12 inches high at the withers, is a very tough and sturdy dog.

Bergamasco

46 • The Bergamasco is rarely seen outside Italy, where it is still used as a sheepdog.

47 • Much patience and expertise is required to tend the Bergamasco's matted coat.

Briard

48 • The Briard is very particular about his friends and is a family dog that is wary of strangers.

49 • The Briard makes an excellent guard dog or sheepdog and tends to have a dominant character.

Bearded Collie

50 • Large curious eyes peep out from beneath the Bearded Collie's thick fringe.

51 • The Bearded Collie is protected by a double coat: the smooth outer one acts as an "umbrella," while the soft, wavy undercoat serves as "padding."

Border Collie

While the attentive, watchful and intelligent Border Collie is a fairly sociable dog, it is not willing to be everyone's friend.

Shetland Sheepdog
(Collie)

- Although the Collie is one of the noblest and proudest-looking dogs, it is actually very gentle and affectionate with its human family and is sometimes so sensitive as to be retiring or nervous.

Bobtail
(Old English Sheepdog)

56 • The Old English Sheepdog was originally bred to tend the flocks, but is also very well suited to agility contests.

57 • It is easy to be tempted to trim the Old English Sheepdog's coat in various ways, for if left long it requires a great deal of grooming.

Bouvier
des Flandres

- The Bouvier des Flandres is a reliable sheepdog and guard dog and also served as an excellent ambulance dog during World War I, when it was used to seek casualties.

Australian Shepherd

● Australian Shepherds are keen to learn and work and should always be kept active.
Many examples have highly variegated coats, with blue, red, white and black patches,
like the dog shown on the right.

Maremma and Abruzzese Sheepdog

62 • The Maremma and Abruzzese Sheepdog is an unerring guardian of flocks and is characterized by its massive head and strong muzzle.

63 • The Maremma and Abruzzese Sheepdog is also an excellent canine "bodyguard" and is very protective towards both its puppies and the members of its human family.

Shar Pei

64 • The loose skin of the Shar Pei makes it one of the most surprising dogs in terms of appearance. The puppies of this breed are particularly heavily wrinkled.

65 • Although the SharPei is not particularly obedient, it is an affectionate and well-balanced dog with an even disposition.

66, 66-67 and 68-69 ● Despite the sagging appearance of its skin, the Shar Pei is a muscular and strongly built breed that was probably originally used as a hunting dog or guard dog in its native China.

Argentine Dogo

70 ● The Argentine Dogo is a brave and determined dog that was bred for hunting.

70-71 ● The Argentine Dogo is well aware of its own strength and rarely needs to bark.

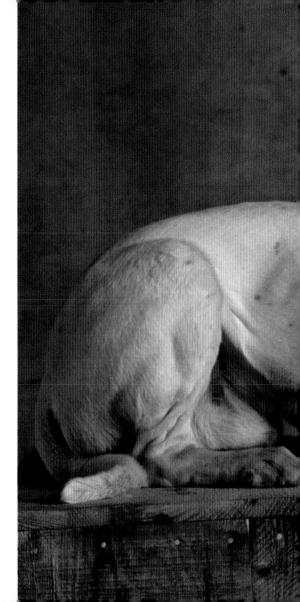

Dogue de Bordeaux

• The Dogue de Bordeaux was bred in France as a guard dog and is very reliable in this role. If one of these dogs should bark at someone, it normally has a very good reason for doing so.

Rottweiler

74 • The Rottweiler is a strong and self-confident dog that is very loyal.

75 • The Rottweiler becomes so deeply attached to its human family that it would readily die to defend it.

Doberman

● The Doberman is one of the most elegantly proportioned dogs.
It is renowned for its loyalty, courage and strength as a guard dog.

78 • A pack of Dobermans undoubtedly makes a striking impression, for these strong-willed dogs are passionately devoted to their family.

79 • The tension of a startled Doberman is palpable. Experience and authority are required to train and educate these dogs, along with calmness and a touch of delicacy.

Schnauzer

80 • The confident gait of this Schnauzer demonstrates the typical composure
of the breed.

81 • The Schnauzer forms a deep bond with its human companions and can suffer
greatly if forced to change owner.

- There are three very different sizes of Schnauzer, measuring between 12 and 27 inches at the withers.

Saint Bernard

84 • The Saint Bernard is one of the largest and heaviest breeds and is a cheerful, stable and very sensitive dog.

85 • This canine giant with its brandy barrel around its neck has become an authentic icon, renowned all over the world for its proven skills as a rescue dog.

● The Saint Bernard's
huge placid-looking
head hints at the
typically calm nature of
the breed, which is
especially evident in
adult dogs.

Neapolitan Mastiff

- The jet-black Neapolitan Mastiff with its blood-red eyes has a diabolical air. While this appearance undoubtedly helps to make it a formidable guard dog, it fails to do justice to the complete loyalty and great affection that the breed shows towards its human family.

Bulldog

90 • The Bulldog long ago lost the fierce disposition of its ancestors and is now one of the gentlest and most dependable breeds.

91 • Despite this "ready to pounce" pose, the Bulldog is an excellent apartment dog and is not particularly fond of the outdoor life or long walks.

92 • While Bulldogs are fairly lively as puppies, they tend to calm down a great deal when they become adults, like this mother with her litter.

93 • The Bulldog's terrible teeth were once its weapons in the days in which the unfortunate animal was used for bullbaiting, which is now banned.

Bernese Mountain Dog

94 • The Bernese Mountain Dog is a dynamic dog that is at home in the snow, making it a versatile breed that is suitable as a rescue or guard dog as well as a herding dog.

95 and 96-97 • The Bernese Mountain Dog's handsome and lively head expresses the breed's great intelligence, which is considered to be above the canine average.

Boxer

98 • Although the Boxer was originally bred as a fighting dog and subsequently as a guard and working dog, it is now one of the most faithful, unaffected and playful companions that a person could choose.

99 • The Boxer's athletic and agile physique make it the ideal companion for sports enthusiasts and those who love the outdoor life.

Great Dane

100, 101 and 102-103 ● The gigantic Great Dane is a powerful and noble dog, but also very playful and sometimes even shy. However, this breed is also very attentive to what goes on around it, making it a good guard dog.

104 • Despite its strength, the Great Dane is fond of comfort and dislikes harsh conditions such as cold weather and rain.

105 • Great Danes are highly sensitive to the human voice and can be very upset by an angry tone.

Bullmastiff

106 • Even when puppies, Bullmastiffs display the breed's typical calm
and peaceful nature.

107 • Curiously, the brave, obedient and solidly built Bullmastiff was bred to protect
and help gamekeepers combat poachers.

Cane Corso

● The Cane Corso will boldly defend its human family.
The origins of the breed can be traced back to ancient Roman times,
when these dogs were the faithful companions of the legionaries.

• The Cane Corso's name is not derived from the island of Corsica, but from its massive frame, which is clearly visible in these photographs: indeed corsu is an ancient word that means "sturdy."

Leonberger

● The Leonberger is a calm and well-balanced dog with an imposing appearance.
It was bred to perform various tasks and its poorly developed hunting instinct makes
it sociable with other animals.

Newfoundland

● Shaggy Newfoundlands are nimbler and more agile then their size suggests.
They were bred to work alongside the fishermen of the Canadian island after which
they were named and love to swim in cold waters whatever the weather.

Fox Terrier

116 • The Fox Terrier's specialty is sticking its whiskery nose wherever anything moves, for it was bred to flush foxes, badgers and vermin out of their dens.

117 • The Fox Terrier is a sociable and resourceful dog that is incredibly determined.

Scottish Terrier and West Highland White Terrier

- Although both the black Scottish Terrier and the West Highland White Terrier were bred to flush out animals such as foxes and hares, they have very different natures. Indeed the former is more reserved, while the latter is livelier and more extroverted.

Norwich
Terrier

• The Norwich Terrier confirms the
saying that the smaller the dog, the more
energetic it is, and indeed Norwich
Terriers are so lively as to seem impudent.

Welsh Terrier

122 • The great Terrier group also includes the Welsh Terrier, a medium-sized dog with a compact and sturdy body.

123 • The watchful Welsh Terrier is a calm and attentive observer and is generally more obedient than the other members of its group.

Lakeland Terrier

• The expression of the Lakeland Terrier betrays its keen intelligence.
These dogs are quick learners and enjoy challenging activities
such as agility contests.

Skye Terrier

- Surprisingly, the Skye Terrier's handsome long coat does not require much grooming; it is the dog's "whiskers" that need most attention and frequent combing.

Yorkshire Terrier

128 • The Yorkshire Terrier is one of the typical show dogs that are carefully groomed and adorned with ribbons.

129 • However, the Yorkshire Terrier's affected show appearance belies its true nature, which is overly fearless – especially towards larger dogs.

130 • Yorkshire Terriers enjoy the outdoor life and have retained their instinct
to hunt small animals, such as field mice.

131 • The hair in front of the Yorkshire Terrier's eyes in usually tied up in a topknot
for casual and elegant occasions alike.

Parson Russell
Terrier

● The Parson Russell Terrier has a particularly unaffected nature, which can even
tend towards mischievousness if overindulged.

Bull Terrier

- The oval head of the Bull Terrier makes this breed easily recognizable. These dogs are practically immune to pain, which makes it essential to carefully monitor their health.

Jagdterrier

136 and 137 ● The Jagdterrier is a true hunter that has been bred to attack larger animals.

138-139 ● A lively Jagdterrier captured during a surprising moment of relaxation.

Australian Terrier

- The Australian Terrier is a small dog with a great personality, which has a tendency towards stubbornness, like most other members of its group. However, it is also very adaptable, both as a working dog and as a companion.

Airedale Terrier

The Airedale Terrier, bred for otter hunting in the 19th century, has also been "enlisted" in various armies as a rescue dog and night watchdog.

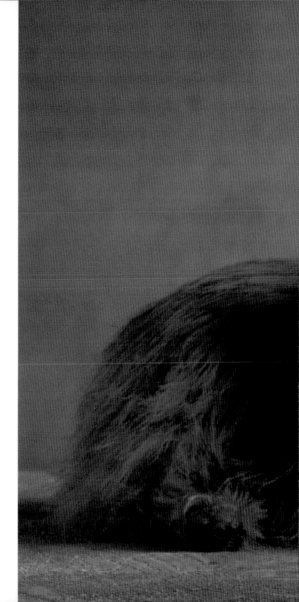

Cairn Terrier

● The Cairn Terrier enjoys participating
in family life, but always retains a pinch
of stubbornness and independence,
even if well trained.

American Staffordshire Terrier

• The American Staffordshire Terrier is an extremely strong dog that is suitable for experienced owners. On the other hand, it is often seen among the winners of obedience competitions.

Pit Bull Terrier

148 • Although much maligned by the popular press, the Pit Bull Terrier is no more aggressive than any other breed, for all dogs will bite if they feel threatened.

149 • The Pit Bull Terrier's name is derived from a barbaric competition that was popular in the United States during the 19th century in which the dogs were thrown into a pit full of rats and the one that killed the greatest number was the winner.

Dandie Dinmont Terrier

- The likeable Dandie Dinmont Terrier (whose name comes from a character in a novel by Sir Walter Scott, who owned one of these dogs) has a calm nature and adapts well to any environment, but is also an excellent hunter of rats and weasels.

Dachshund

● The Dachshund is a magnificent companion and hunting dog that has a double personality, for it is brave and tireless in the field as well as a cuddly pet that is very sensitive to the moods of humans at home. The wirehaired variety is shown here.

154-155 ● This longhaired Dachshund with a bright chestnut coat expresses well the dignity of the breed.

156-157 ● The shorthaired Dachshund is the original type of this breed.

Samoyed

- The Samoyed is a medium-sized white Arctic Spitz breed that originated in Siberia and Northern Russia. Its typical expression is known as the "Samoyed smile."

Greenland Dog

- The Greenland Dog is a sturdy breed with a wide head, thick neck and small triangular ears. Its front legs are strong and straight, while the back ones are slightly sloping. These characteristics make it ideally suited to pulling sleds and to the harsh Arctic conditions of its homeland.

Akita Inu

● The Akita Inu is a large, powerfully built dog that is a native of the Japanese island of Honshu. It is docile with its owner, but often wary of those whom it considers hostile.

Karelian Bear Dog

The Karelian Bear Dog originated in Finland and the Russian region of Karelia. It is a medium-sized Spitz breed with a long body and a thick coat. It has a well-balanced and playful nature, while its refined sense of smell makes it ideal for hunting.

Alaskan Malamute

- The Alaskan Malamute hails from the area between Alaska and Greenland. Its name derives from the fact that it was once bred by the Mahlemiut Inuit tribe.

Siberian Husky

168, 169 and 170-171 • The Siberian Husky is a sturdily built dog with a soft outer coat and a woolly undercoat. It is a playful and affectionate breed that is also very independent.

Chow Chow

The Chow Chow originated in Asia. Its very thick red coat and dark tongue – a rarity among mammals – make it an unmistakable breed.

Pomeranian

- The Pomeranian takes its name from the old Prussian region where it was bred. It is a Spitz breed with a maximum height of 12 inches and a long, thick coat.

Basset Hound

- The Basset Hound was officially recognized in 1883. This breed has a long, low-set body and distinctive droopy ears.

* The Basset Hound is a very placid dog that is utterly incapable of biting and loves to be petted.

Bloodhound

- The Bloodhound's origins go back almost 1,000 years, when the breed was probably developed by Belgian monks. It is a medium-sized dog with a large black nose, long ears and a very docile nature.

Basset
Artésien-Normand

- The Basset Artésien-Normand does not exceed 14 inches in height, although its body tends to be twice as long. It has long, pointed ears.

Beagle

- The Beagle is a mild-mannered and very friendly dog, as suggested by its appearance and expression. Although it is practically never aggressive, it was actually bred for hunting, and despite becoming very fond of its human family, it also enjoys life in the pack.

Grand Basset Vendéen

- Thanks to its smaller size, this breed, derived from the Grand Griffon Vendéen, is ideal for flushing and chasing quarry. It has a long body and a long, wiry coat.

Dalmatian

188, 189 and 190-191 ● The Dalmatian has very ancient origins, which are difficult to trace precisely. The distinctive feature of the breed is its white coat with black or brown spots.

Epagneul Bréton

● The Epagneul Bréton has a thick, flat
coat with two or three different colors and
short, rounded ears. Its size, which does
not generally exceed 20 inches in height,
makes it a sought-after gundog.

German Shorthaired Pointer

- The German Shorthaired Pointer was developed in Germany in the 19th century by crossing various breeds. Its great versatility in the field makes it an excellent gundog.

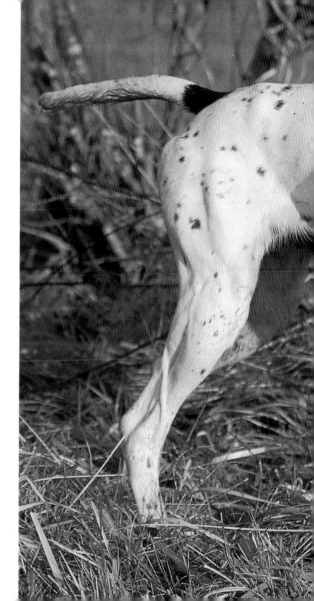

Pointer

- The Pointer has an elegant gait and is a skilled hunting dog that is particularly good at pointing, hence its name.

Gordon Setter

- The Gordon Setter is named after the Duke of Gordon, who started to develop the breed in 1820. It is a strong and sturdy gundog that is capable of working both on land and in the water. This Setter has a medium-length and sometimes slightly wavy black coat with tan markings and feathering on the ears and the lower part of the body.

English Setter
and
Irish Setter

200-201 • The English Setter is a gundog with a silky tricolor or white coat with black, orange, liver or lemon markings.

201 • The Irish Setter has a long muzzle and a large black nose.

- The Irish Setter is an energetic gundog. Its long coat can be either all red or red and white.

Wirehaired Pointing Griffon

- The distinguishing feature of the Wirehaired Pointing Griffon, developed at the turn of the 19th century by the Dutch breeder Korthal, is its bushy eyebrows and heavy whiskers.

Bracco Italiano

- The Bracco Italiano has been known since the times of Xenophon and has a short white coat spotted with orange or brown. The distinctive features of this breed are its droopy lips, amber eyes and low-set, slightly crumpled ears. The Bracco Italiano is an excellent gundog, but also a great companion.

Weimaraner

- The most striking
thing about the
Weimaraner is its
unusual grey coat with
glints of silver. The dog
has a well-developed
chest, a moderately
tucked-up flank,
muscular hindquarters
and long, straight front
legs. It is very popular
with hunters.

210 • The Weimaraner was developed during the 19th century as a companion and hunting dog for the noblemen of the Grand Duchy of Weimar and is an active, determined and intelligent breed.

211 • The forehead and muzzle of the Weimaraner are of equal length and the dog has long, folded ears and gray or amber eyes.

Cocker Spaniel

The Cocker Spaniel is the smallest gundog and was confused with the English Cocker Spaniel until the two breeds were definitively separated in 1941. It has a compact, sturdy body and long, well-feathered ears. It can reach considerable speeds and maintain them over long distances.

English Cocker Spaniel

- The English Cocker Spaniel was developed during the 19th century and soon became one of the most popular breeds in Europe. This lively dog is used to flush and retrieve game, but also makes a perfect pet. Its head is particularly large in relation to the size of its body and its large nose has a highly refined sense of smell.

Golden Retriever

● The Golden Retriever was developed in Scotland during the 19th century, but its origins were not recognized by the British Kennel Club until 1960. It is a sturdy dog with a straight outer coat and a dense, waterproof undercoat. It is friendly and requires an outdoor space for exercise. Along with the Labrador, this is the best-known of the Retriever breeds.

Labrador Retriever

218, 219 and 220-221 ● The Labrador is the most familiar Retriever and was introduced to the island of Newfoundland in the 19th century by British ships that reached it from the Canadian Labrador peninsula. It is a hardy dog and although not particularly fast, it has great muscular power. Indeed, it was bred as a gundog for the tiring and lengthy task of retrieving waterfowl.

● The Labrador has a short, stiff coat, with a waterproof undercoat and a layer of subcutaneous fat that protects it from the cold. Its mono-colored coat may be one of three different colors: black, chocolate or tawny.

English Springer Spaniel

- The English Springer Spaniel has a compact body and is able to cover ground rapidly.
It is used to hunt game, which it flushes out for shooting.

Epagneul Nain
Papillon

• The Papillon owes its name to its large, erect, fringed ears that resemble a butterfly's wings.

Little Lion Dog
(Löwchen)

• The Löwchen, which means "little lion" in German, originated in the Renaissance, when it became widespread as an "exotic animal" among the ladies of the European courts. Typically, certain parts of the dog's body are generally clipped for cosmetic reasons.

Shih Tzu

● Despite its small size, this dog, which originated in China, is very strong. One of its distinctive features is the hair above its nose, which grows in an upward direction.

Bolognese

- The Bolognese has very ancient origins and was the "aristocratic" dog of the nobility for many centuries. The breed was saved after having risked dying out in the mid 20th century.

French Bulldog

- The French Bulldog is probably derived
from its English cousin. This small,
smooth-haired dog with a very short
muzzle is intelligent and dynamic,
but also rather lazy.

Pug

- The muscular, compact Pug is a very old Chinese breed whose short, wrinkled muzzle and large, round eyes give it a comic expression. Its short, heavy-set body gives it a stocky appearance.

Poodle

238, 239 and 240-241 • For many centuries the Poodle was one of the best-loved dogs of aristocrats and noble families. Its distinctive curly coat requires careful clipping.

Chinese Crested

- There are two main types of Chinese Crested: the hairy Powderpuff and the Hairless. The latter has hair only on the head, legs and tail.

The Powderpuff" variety, on the other hand, has a long, silky coat. Both varieties of the Chinese Crested are shy and easily startled.

Cavalier King Charles Spaniel

246-247 • The history of the Cavalier King Charles Spaniel is associated with that of the English aristocracy. Following World War I, the breed risked dying out and was revived by several English dog-fanciers.

248-249 • The Chihuahua is a record-breaking dog, the smallest and lightest of the canine family (1–6 pounds).

Chihuahua

Maltese

- The Maltese did not originate in Malta, but in the countries of the central Mediterranean area and was already known during Aristotle's time. The breed is small but very elegant, due to its long frame and very long coat that hides its body. When it runs, the dog appears to glide over the ground.

Pekingese

252, 252-253 and 254-255
For many centuries the Pekingese
was the dog of the Chinese
imperial family and was imported
to Europe around 1860. Its
distinguishing features are its small
size, large eyes, flattened muzzle
and long, straight coat.

Borzoi

● The Borzoi is sometimes referred to as the "Russian Greyhound" and is a large dog with a thick coat and particularly elongated features. This breed has a calm and very self-possessed nature.

Greyhound

258, 259 and 260-261 • The Greyhound is probably descended from oriental sight hounds and appears in various European paintings from the 16th century onward. It is a medium-sized dog with a very muscular but lean body, which enables it to achieve great speeds. One of the distinguishing features of the breed is its very gentle nature.

Afghan Hound

• The Afghan Hound is a dog
with ancient and possibly Middle
Eastern origins, a long, narrow
muzzle and a long, coat and ears.
Its coat may be chestnut, black,
white or three-colored.

Azawakh

● The Azawakh comes from the valley of the same name in the Nigerian Basin, where nomadic tribes keep it as a working dog and companion. Its skeleton and lean musculature are clearly visible beneath its skin.

IRRESISTIBLE MADCAPS

- Play is essential part of growing up for this Rottweiler puppy.

INTRODUCTION Irresistible Madcaps

THERE IS NO BETTER WAY TO DELVE INTO THE CANINE SPIRIT THAN TO OBSERVE A PUPPY DURING THE SHORT TIME IN WHICH ITS LIFE IS ENTIRELY DEPENDENT ON THEIR RELATIONS WITH ITS MOTHER, ITS SIBLINGS AND FINALLY ITS FATHER. IT SPENDS THIS TIME EXPERIMENTING BEHAVIORAL PATTERNS THAT HAVE JUST TWO PURPOSES: SURVIVAL AND LEARNING TO LIVE WITH OTHERS. THIS PERIOD IS BRIEF BECAUSE PUPPIES GROW FAST AND ADAPT TO THEIR SURROUNDINGS FROM THE MOMENT THAT THEY ARE BORN, ALBEIT WITH MOTOR AND VISUAL LIMITATIONS. THE PUPPY SWAYS ITS HEAD AS IT MOVES, SEEKING THE PROTECTIVE EMBRACE OF ITS MOTHER AND HER TEAT, TO WHICH IT CLINGS EVEN WHEN SLEEPING, FOR FEAR OF LOSING IT. IT PUSHES WITH ITS REAR PAWS TO ENSURE IT-

INTRODUZIONE Irresistible Madcaps

SELF THE MOST REASSURING PLACE AMONG THE FOLDS

OF ITS MOTHER'S BODY OR AMID ITS SIBLINGS. IT NEVER

MOVES IN A STRAIGHT LINE, BUT IN CIRCLES, TO AVOID THE

RISK OF STRAYING AWAY FROM COMFORTABLE UNIVERSE

THAT IS ITS WHOLE WORLD, ITS SALVATION AND ITS ONLY

REASON FOR LIVING. NOW THE PUPPY BELONGS TO ITS

MOTHER AND NOBODY ELSE. ITS SIBLINGS ACT IN THE

SAME WAY, MOVING TOWARDS THE WARMTH, EATING AND

SLEEPING. IF FOR A MOMENT THE PUPPY FEELS LOST OR

DEFEATED, A YELP IS ENOUGH TO MAKE THE MOTHER

COME. WHAT PATIENCE SHE HAS! SHE SPENDS ALMOST

ALL HER TIME LYING DOWN TO COMFORT, SUCKLE AND

CLEAN HER PUPPIES WITH ENERGETIC LICKING. THE FA-

THER KEEPS HIS DISTANCE, BUT WATCHES OVER HIS FAMI-

Irresistible Madcaps

Introduction

LY, LIMITING HIMSELF TO NOSING AND CASTING LANGUID GLANCES AT THEIR MOTHER. BUT THE PUPPIES GROW QUICKLY, SO COMES THE TIME TO LEARN TO LIVE WITH OTHERS. THE PUPPY GAIN THIS EXPERIENCE BY PLAYING FIGHTS WITH ITS SIBLINGS, IN A SUCCESSION OF NIPPING AND BEING NIPPED, IN WHICH EACH BECOMES AWARE OF ITS STRENGTH AND THE STRENGTH OF OTHERS, THUS ACQUIRING THE SENSE OF PROPORTION. THE FATHER NOW REALIZES THAT IT IS TIME TO EXPLAIN THE RULES, INVITING THE PUPPIES TO PLAY AND STOPPING THEM WHEN THEY GO TOO FAR. AS ALWAYS IN NATURE, PLAY IS NOT AN END UNTO ITSELF BUT THE BEST WAY FOR THE FATHER TO TEACH HIS PUPPIES THE LIMITS THAT MUST BE RESPECTED.

- Puppies have disproportionately large heads, as demonstrated by this Bernese Mountain Dog pup.

272 • A Boxer intent on chewing his bone – an essential exercise for reinforcing his teeth.

273 • A Basset Hound tries out his young teeth on a branch.

66 THE FIRST WEEKS OF A PUPPY'S LIFE ARE CRUCIAL AND UNREPEATABLE: THIS IS THE TIME IN WHICH HE MUST LEARN TO SOCIALIZE, THUS BECOMING A TRUE COMPANION FOR HIS HUMAN FAMILY. IF HE IS TAUGHT WITH PATIENCE AND FIRMNESS, LIKE A CHILD, THE PUPPY WILL LEARN TO LIVE IN PERFECT HARMONY WITH HIS NEW WORLD. 99

• A Golden Retriever puppy divides his waking hours between play and exploring his surroundings with his sense of smell.

A young Beagle exploring the natural world. This breed is particularly lively.

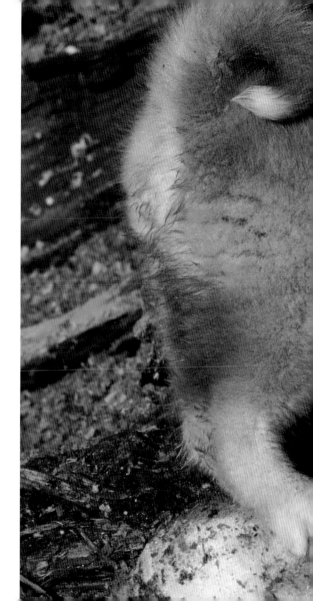

- Something beneath the dry bark has caught the attention of this young Chow Chow, who is perfectly at home in cold weather.

● Two Border Collies intent on playing. Play is just as important for their development as it is for that of children. This intelligent breed is exceptionally obedient.

● Playful Border Collie puppies compete with each other for a mock prey.

284-285 • A "tug of war" puts the resistance of this pair of 12-week-old Border Collies to the test.

286-287 • It is essential to give a puppy like this Terrier his own toys, for without these colored balls, his attention could easily turn to the sofa...

● Objects like balls and rubber bones are artificial "quarries" that allow puppies to channel their hunting instinct, which most modern dogs are no longer able to put to practical use.

● Labrador Retrievers are simply irrepressible puppies that love chewing things – and not just a rubber bone or their littermates' ears – and are renowned for destroying sofas, chairs, shoes and anything within range.

A young black crossbreed makes the most of running free in the fields. Crossbreeds are generally very intelligent and sound, but nonetheless require proper training.

• A Border Collie carefully studies
the best way to quench his thirst.

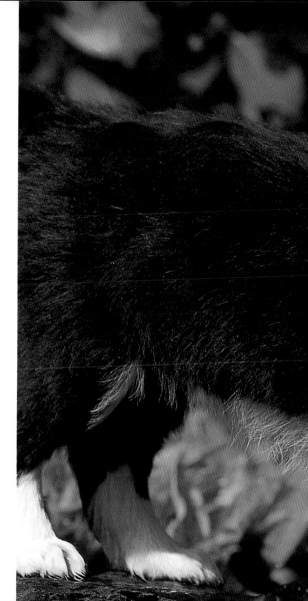

296, 297 and 298-299 • Puppies are curious and attentive and love to sit on the sidelines and watch.

300 • A young Labrador Retriever enjoys his freedom. Puppies are able to keep their instincts alive if they are allowed contact with nature.

301 • A Dalmatian puppy has trouble controlling himself, for each stimulus is an excuse to do something and avoid boredom.

302 ● A vehement dispute
between two Saint Bernard
puppies. This breed has a strong
tendency to dominate.

302-303 ● Any moving object
(especially if it does not react) is
either a quarry or a toy.

This Border Collie puppy has only had a couple of months of experience in getting to grips with nature and is interested in whatever surprises him, which is practically everything.

A "friendly giant" among the grass and flowers. The Great Dane is a breed that is very fond of human company.

" Each puppy has its own distinct personality: it may be dominant or remissive, or show a balance of these two characteristics. It is important to try to sense the puppy's character in order to understand what kind of dog it will be as an adult and which kinds of behavior must be corrected. "

• This slightly clumsy-looking Bracco Italiano puppy actually belongs to a very athletic, agile and powerful breed.

310 and 311 • A rare quiet moment for two Parson Russell Terrier puppies. This breed is usually lively and can sometimes be rather self-assertive towards other male dogs.

312-313 • A Bolognese puppy enjoys having his back scratched.

314 ● A handsome Bernese Mountain Dog puppy: this breed is popular both for its fine appearance and for its working skills and forms a very close bond with its human companions.

315 ● Gundogs like this Bracco Italiano are relatively "composed" even when puppies, when they are active but not excitable.

• After a while play and exploration take their toll and give way to yawns. Puppies (two Dachshunds, left, and a pair of Parson Russell Terriers, right) quickly use up their energy.

● Powerful paws trample the snow: Saint Bernards, are imposing dogs even when puppies and possess a strong personality.

● The sense of smell is very precious for puppies like the Wirehaired Pointing Griffon, left, and the Golden Retriever, right, who are engrossed in the inspection of flowers.

" **P**UPPIES POSSESS AN UNDELIBERATE AND LIVELY AWKWARDNESS AND HAVE TO LEARN EVERYTHING THAT IS NOT INSTINCTIVE TO THEM, BUT THEY ALSO HAVE MUCH TO OFFER THOSE WHO LOVE THEM AND TRAIN THEM. IF THEY ARE NOT TRAINED, THEN THEY WILL NOT BE SUITED TO ANY KIND OF ENVIRONMENT OR COMPANIONSHIP, AND WILL THUS BE DESTINED FOR AN UNHAPPY LIFE. "

● These two six-week-old Staffordshire Bull Terriers are full of life, but the one on the left seems bolder. Indeed, not all dogs of the same breed share the same character.

Dalmatians at play. These dogs are brimming with energy and fully live up to their movie fame.

● Even when engrossed in play, it takes very little to distract a puppy: the little Cocker Spaniel lying on his back has just noticed the photographer.

"Each puppy has its own personality, which nonetheless falls within the typical behavior of its breed. Consequently, when choosing a puppy, it is not only essential to be aware of its dietary and health needs, but also those regarding its nature in terms of companionship and social relations."

• These Lakeland Terrier/Border Collie cross puppies express themselves in playful attacks.

"NATURE MUST ALWAYS STRUGGLE AGAINST ITSELF TO SURVIVE, AND THIS IS REFLECTED IN ANIMAL BEHAVIOR FROM A VERY EARLY AGE. FOLLOWING WEANING, NO PUPPY IS ABLE TO RESIST THE INSTINCT TO ESTABLISH HIERARCHIES AND THUS CONFER AN ESSENTIAL SENSE OF ORDER ON ITS WORLD."

• A pair of six-week-old Springer Spaniels enjoy a play fight, but the aim of the game is still to subdue the opponent.

These German Shepherd puppies belong to a recent breed (1889) that is renowned for its intelligence and patience, but requires firm training.

334 ❋ A Pembroke Welsh Corgi puppy displays the good nature and intelligence typical of its breed.

335 ❋ This small, comical Yorkshire Terrier puppy with its ruffled coat, will become a brave dog with a strong personality.

336 • This Rottweiler puppy is already very attentive to what is going on about him, as he scans his surroundings.

337 • Parson Russell Terriers are very sensitive as puppies and may panic if left alone.

338 • The Samoyed is already strong and determined as a puppy and is a keenly intelligent and sensitive dog. Indeed, it is best not to shout when scolding him, but to try to convince him instead.

339 • This compact and energetic young Saint Bernard is quite at home in the snow.

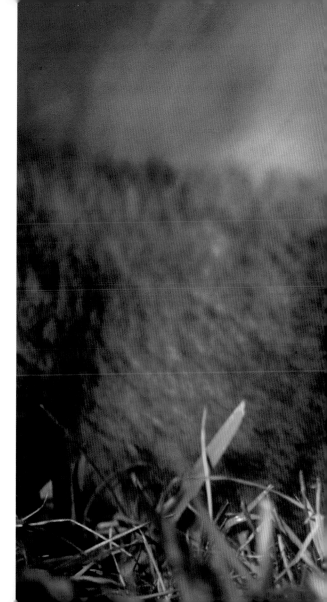

- The Chow Chow is calmer and more obedient than other breeds as a puppy, but appearances can be deceiving, for it becomes far more independent as an adult and will dominate its owner if not firmly trained.

As a puppy, the Bracco Italiano already displays the powerful build that is typical of this intelligent and quick-witted breed.

The gentle eyes and calm stance of this puppy belies the fierce reputation of the Pit Bull Terrier. A dog's behavior is largely dependent on the type of training that it receives.

346 ● Two Alaskan Malamutes exploring. This breed is only really happy when running free.

346-347 ● Two Labrador Retriever puppies argue over a stick. These dogs are born retrievers that love to chase and bring back objects.

348 • Two Polish Lowland Sheepdog puppies study each other with their noses. This breed is generally sociable with other animals, but more reticent with people.

349 • Bichon Frise puppies are bright and playful, and practically never aggressive.

350 and 350-351 • Their loose skin often gives Bracco Italiano puppies a comical, perpetually "thoughtful" look.

352-353 • A fine selection of Retriever puppies: two black Labradors and three Golden Retrievers "pose" for a group photograph.

Puppies' days are an
alternating succession
of waking and sleeping
hours. The photograph
shows three Border
Collies, which are
particularly active
working dogs.

A Boxer puppy rests among the flowers. Puppies only have a limited store of energy and every now and then they have to stop to "charge their batteries."

• A brick wall or a fence: for puppies everything that lies beyond an obstacle is worthy of exploration and instead of holding them back, their inexperience only seems to urge them on.

A Parson Russell Terrier and a
Border Collie get to grips with soft
and colorful toys. Studies have
shown that dogs can see colors in
the spectrum from purple to
yellow, but not red and orange.

362 and 363 ● A Parson Russell Terrier puppy dedicates his complete attention to a dry stick. Terriers in general retain a strong natural instinct and can be rather stubborn when they make up their minds to do something.

364-365 ● A litter of Labrador Retrievers poses for the photographer during an unusually calm moment.

It is easy to observe when a puppy (a Pointer, left, and a Bulldog, right) wants to be sure that he has understood what he has been told.

The absorbed expressions of these two puppies (Labrador, left, and Borzoi, right) reveal the attention that dogs dedicate to trying to understand what is required of them.

• There is nothing that energetic
Labrador puppies like more than a
good romp, but they also enjoy a
quiet moment with their bone.

The droopy eared and furrow-browed Basset Hound is a peaceful and gentle breed, but is not an easy dog to train and can sometimes be rather stubborn.

374 • The yawns of this little Springer Spaniel's littermate appear to be more intriguing than contagious.

375 • Two Siberian Husky puppies "converse" in one of the many ways used by dogs, whose language is based on sight, hearing, smell and the interpretation of instinctive behavior.

376 • Two little Dalmatians yawn in unison. The yawning mechanism is triggered by more or less the same sensations in all mammals: hunger, tiredness or boredom, and sometimes – particularly in the case of dogs – nervousness.

377 • Two Cavalier King Charles Spaniels nip each other. Puppies are reassured by this kind of behavior, which they learn from their mother.

A puppy's life: two Border Collies (left) and a pair of Springer Spaniels (above), caught in a moment of absolute tranquility.

380 • These Bulldog puppies look as though they are scheming something.

381 • Three young Great Danes scrutinize a world that for them is basically based on the laws inherited from their wolf ancestors.

382 • A young Beagle puts his sense of smell to the test among the dry leaves. This breed is very fond of the outdoor life, which does not make it suitable as an apartment dog.

383 • Basset Hounds are not great lovers of activity and their placid appearance seems to emphasize this fact.

These two photographs illustrate two extremes in terms of the variety of dog breeds: a pair of Bull Terriers, with their distinctive egg-shaped heads, above, and a couple of Briards, right.

The coat of long-haired puppies, like these three Spaniels, requires frequent and thorough brushing, especially following a day outdoors.

These sturdy backs belong to three Chinese Shar-Pei puppies. This breed of dog is exceptionally devoted to their human family.

• An inquisitive Great Dane puppy learns about his surroundings,
to which he dedicates the great attention typical of this intelligent and sensitive breed,
which also has an excellent memory.

Effusions between Bloodhounds: these dogs are so sweet-natured
as to tolerate almost anything from children, but may not be so
accommodating with dogs of their own sex.

The Pit Bull Terrier is often the victim of stereotypes, but is an affectionate dog, especially with puppies.

The questioning gaze of this young Basset Hound reveals the breed's sensitivity and intelligence.

Patient mothers and demanding puppies: a handsome pair of Gordon Setters, above, and two Beagles, right.

Beagles are untiring even when puppies and are among the most energetic and active dogs, capable of running and playing for hours on end before stopping.

● Brief moments of calm are interspersed with bursts of liveliness and affection for these Bracco Italiano puppies photographed with their mother.

Puppies know only too well how to succeed in gaining attention: they give no respite.

406 • Despite his inconsolable air, this Basset Hound puppy is actually perfectly happy alongside his mother.

407 • A Briard puppy trustingly approaches his mother, who belongs to a very protective breed.

"Much patience is required with puppies, but nature waits for nobody. Consequently, a puppy's character must be formed according to nature's own schedules, without any traumatic experiences or contradictory messages. This is vital because it is extremely difficult to modify a dog's personality once it has been formed, just as it is for humans."

• An Alaskan Malamute puppy plays with his mother. These dogs have strong personalities and require constant training from an early age.

● Never stray too far! This rule also seems to be valid for these Mastiff puppies, which are still too small to be independent.

This Australian Cattle Dog puppy, still with his mother, will become a brave and adventurous dog.

This young Leonberger is attracted by water. This intelligent breed is fond of human company and has a strong instinct as a rescue dog.

- There is no corner that is not worthy of exploration – even the jaws of this Great Dane.

418 ● This play fight between Golden Retriever puppies is imbued with all the seriousness required by this kind of instinctive confrontation.

419 ● These two German Pinscher puppies are engaged in a bloodless struggle. However, once they become adults, it will be necessary to curb their tendency to fight with other dogs.

● Two Australian Shepherd puppies, with the breed's characteristic multicolored coat, tackle each other with the typical boundless energy of these untiring dogs.

422-423 ● Parson Russell Terrier puppies engaged in a play fight.

423 ● A Parson Russell Terrier puppy observes the camera with a questioning and intrigued gaze.

The "critical" eye of adults helps puppies, in this case a Lowland Polish Sheepdog (above) and an Alaskan Malamute (right), to discover the world by following their examples.

FOUR LEGGED DREAMS

- Two sleeping Cavalier King Charles Spaniels with Blenheim coat (chestnut markings on a pearly white ground) use each other's body as cushions.

INTRODUCTION Four-Legged Dreams

Dogs' SLEEPING HABITS VARY GREATLY FROM IN-
DIVIDUAL TO INDIVIDUAL, FROM PUPPY TO ADULT AND
FROM BREED TO BREED. PUPPIES ALMOST SEEM ADDICT-
ED TO SLEEP, AND NO FUN IN THE WORLD CAN KEEP THEM
AWAKE WHEN THEY ARE TIRED – THEY JUST KEEL OVER.
THEY HAVE PLAYED TOO LONG WITH THEIR BROTHERS
AND SISTERS, MOTHER AND FATHER OR ALL THE MEM-
BERS OF THEIR NEW FAMILY IN TURN AND CANNOT KEEP
THEIR EYES OPEN ANY LONGER. THEY FALL INTO A DEEP
SLEEP, WITHOUT WAITING FOR DARKNESS OR SILENCE
AND DO NOT EVEN CHANGE THEIR MINDS IF YOU PICK
THEM UP BECAUSE YOU WANT TO PLAY WITH THEM A LIT-
TLE LONGER. THEY FALL "AS A DEAD BODY FALLS," TO USE
THE WORDS OF DANTE. YOU CAN TRY SHAKING THEM,

INTRODUCTION Four-Legged Dreams

INVITING THEM TO PLAY OR PLACING A BOWL OF THEIR FAVORITE FOOD BENEATH THEIR NOSES, BUT NONE OF THESE APPROACHES WILL HAVE ANY EFFECT BECAUSE THEY HAVE DECIDED TO SLEEP, AND SLEEP THEY WILL! OVERCOME BY THE TOUCHING SIGHT OF THEIR EXHAUSTED BODIES AND DROWSY AIR, YOU WILL LEAVE THEM TO SLEEP, SPELLBOUND AS YOU WATCH THEM RECOVER THEIR ENERGY, ENCHANTED BY THEIR SPRAWLING FORMS. ADULT DOGS HAVE DIFFERENT SLEEPING HABITS AND RARELY FALL INTO A DEEP SLEEP. THEY FEEL THE BURDEN OF THE RESPONSIBILITY OF THE FAMILY, WORK AND THE THINGS THAT THEY KNOW ARE ENTRUSTED TO THEIR CARE. THEY ARE, IN SHORT, MORE WATCHFUL, TO THE POINT THAT SOME DOGS GIVE THE IMPRESSION THAT

Four-Legged Dreams

Introduction

THEY NEVER SLEEP, JUST DOZE. INDEED, YOU SEE THEM SPRING TO THEIR FEET AT EVERY LITTLE MOVEMENT OR NOISE, SNIFF TO CAPTURE EACH TRACE THAT COULD REVEAL AN INTRUDER AND PRICK THEIR EARS AT THE SLIGHTEST RUSTLE THAT IS NOT CAUSED BY THE WIND. IF YOU LOOK AT THEM, THEY WILL NOT MISS THE CHANCE TO TELL YOU THAT THEY ARE ALERT, WITH A COUPLE OF WAGS OF THEIR TAIL. DO DOGS DREAM? BOTH PUPPIES AND ADULTS DREAM. NOBODY WILL EVER KNOW EXACTLY WHAT ABOUT, BUT WHEN YOU HEAR AND SEE THEM YELPING, WHINING, GROWLING, SHAKING AND EVEN SMILING WHILE SLEEPING, YOU WILL BE ABLE TO CAPTURE THE MEANING OF THEIR DREAMS, FEARS AND DESIRES.

- The Shi Tzu's body is hidden by its long smooth coat, particularly when it lies down.

• These yawning puppies – Border Collie (above) and Labrador Retriever (right) – are characterized by the same upturned noses, closed eyes and wide-open mouths.

434 • A Cavalier King Charles Spaniel dozes, suspended between wakefulness and sleep.

435 • The expression of another Cavalier King Charles Spaniel resembles a yawn.

Sleep AND IN PARTICULAR THE DREAMS THAT AC-COMPANY IT ARE NOT JUST THE PREROGATIVES OF MAN, FOR DOGS TOO SUCCUMB TO THEIR LURE, WHIMPERING, STRETCHING THEIR LEGS AND ASSUMING THE STRANGEST POSITIONS.

• A Parson Russell Terrier and an American Staffordshire Terrier caught yawning.

A Belgian Sheepdog catches his breath, mouth wide open.

440 • Crouching in a field, this West Highland White Terrier is unable to stifle a yawn.

441 • This Dalmatian's yawns reveal how tired he is.

442 ● A sleeping puppy rests on a board as if it were a comfortable cushion.

443 ● A puppy and a wild piglet rest on a bed of leaves.

444 • A sleeping puppy enjoys the warmth of the sun on the wooden boards that he has chosen as his bed.

445 • A tin bucket makes an excellent bed for this snoozing puppy.

446 • Although lying on his back, this sleeping Parson Russell Terrier does not lose his balance.

447 • A mongrel/Schnauzer cross rests in a sitting position.

The unmistakable Basset Hound with his long, droopy ears, lingers in a state of drowsiness.

450 • This Beagle has fallen asleep with his front legs stretched out.

450-451 • This Bloodhound's gaze clearly betrays his sleepiness.

452 and 453 • The Bloodhound's crumpled face gives the breed a sleepy air.

454-455 • A Bloodhound enjoys the relaxing effect of the soft grass.

456 and 457 • These Bullmastiff puppies lean against the sides of their basket as if it were a soft cushion.

458-459 • Two Bulldogs take advantage of their soft bodies to cushion their weight upon the hard floor, just as though they were lying on a mattress.

460-461 ● These two Dalmatians and the cat lying between them seem to belong to the same litter.

462-463 ● A young Belgian Sheepdog sleeps with his head buried between his paws.

464 • A plastic bone serves as a comfortable pillow for these two Labrador Retriever puppies.

465 • A Border Collie relaxes, stretching his legs and resting his head on the ground.

466-467 • The "crumpled" face of the Chinese Shar-Pei becomes even more creased during sleep, when he rests his massive head on the ground.

● Whether viewed from the front (right) or from the side (left), this young Bulldog has the breed's typical knowing expression.

" LIKE PEOPLE, DOGS CAN BE DYNAMIC OR LAZY, CONSTANTLY ALERT OR SLEEPYHEADS CERTAIN BREEDS, SUCH AS BULLDOGS, ARE FAIRLY RELAXED AND SLEEP A LOT, WHILE OTHERS, SUCH AS GREYHOUNDS OR DALMATIANS, ARE PARTICULARLY ACTIVE. DOGS SLEEP FOR AROUND TEN HOURS A DAY. "

470 • A Cocker Spaniel lies lazily on the floor.

471 • A Bulldog rests his heavy head on his paws while he sleeps.

472 and 473 • Bullmastiff puppies seem to have an overabundance of loose skin in relation to their small bodies, which gives them a comical appearance, especially when they sleep.

474-475 • Alaskan Malamute puppies sleep huddled together.

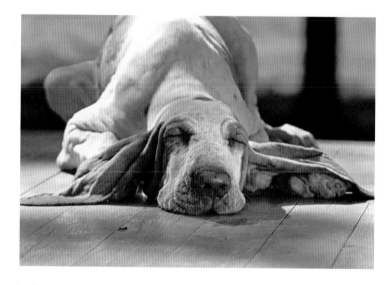

476 • The face of this sleeping Bracco Italiano is characterized by his long ears covering his paws, his large nose and his tightly closed eyes.

477 • Like all babies, most of the time the have their eyes closed, like the one shown.

478-479 • A Beagle takes a rest on some wooden boards, tail, ears and legs dangling.

480-481 • Siberian Huskies are perfectly happy to lie on icy or snowy ground, for their thick coats protect them from the harshest weather conditions.

481 • Siberian Huskies are used as sled dogs in the northern lands, and often have to make extenuating journeys. Once they reach their destination, they fall asleep, exhausted.

482 • A Labrador puppy seeks the protection of a blanket for a siesta.

483 • A puppy lets himself be rocked by the swaying movement of a hammock.

484-485 • Two Siberian Huskies sleep snuggled up against each other.

486 • This Bulldog's sleep is so heavy it seems to flatten his body against the floor.

487 • A Bernese Mountain Dog is about to succumb to the temptation of sleep.

488-489 • A litter takes a nap.

WILD RELATIVES

A race between two young Gray Wolves: these wild relatives of the dog love to play with members of their pack at all ages.

INTRODUCTION Wild Relatives

THERE ARE AROUND 250 WILD RELATIVES OF THE DOG BELONGING TO THE SPECIES AND SUBSPECIES OF THE CANIDAE FAMILY. THIS BIG FAMILY HAS PREFERRED THE PATH OF NATURAL EVOLUTION TO THAT OF COEVOLUTION WITH MAN. HOWEVER, DOGS HAVE NOT FORGOTTEN THEIR NEAREST RELATIONS, DESPITE THE GREAT MANIPULATION WORKED BY MAN ON THEIR BODIES AND CHARACTERS. WE CAN BE SEEN BY LOOKING MORE CLOSELY AT THEIR WILD RELATIVES THAT, INDEED, DOMESTIC DOGS HAVE NOT ONLY PRESERVED THE APPEARANCE OF THE WILD DOGS, BUT ALSO THEIR INSTINCTS, TRADITIONS, SOCIAL RELATIONS, BEHAVIOR PATTERNS AND, IN PARTICULAR, DEVOTION TO THE FAMILY AND PACK AND CONCEPT OF HIERARCHY WITHIN THE

INTRODUCTION

GROUP TO WHICH THEY BELONG. A DOG THAT HOWLS, FURIOUSLY WAVES A SLIPPER GRIPPED TIGHTLY BE-TWEEN ITS TEETH, RUNS AFTER AN OBJECT THAT HAS BEEN THROWN FOR IT, LIES ON ITS BACK BEFORE US, ROLLS ON THE GROUND OR BUMPS AGAINST US WITH ITS HINDQUARTERS OR NOSE, IS MERELY SHOWING US ITS FAMILY PHOTOS. AND INDEED, HOW MANY TIMES HAVE WE OURSELVES PROUDLY STATED THAT OUR FOUR-LEGGED FRIEND LOOKS LIKE A WOLF? ALTHOUGH IT IS TRUE THAT THE SIMILARITY WITH THE CANIDS MORE READILY COMES TO MIND WHEN WE WISH TO EMPHASIZE OUR COMPANIONS' COURAGE, STRENGTH OR CUNNING-NESS, RATHER THAN FEARS, TENDERNESS WITH PUPPIES OR EXTRAORDINARY SOCIABILITY, IT IS ONLY BECAUSE

Wild Relatives

Introduction

WE HAVE NEVER PAID MUCH ATTENTION TO THEIR CLOSE RELATIVES. THIS IS PARTLY DUE TO THE DIFFICULTY OF CONTACT, BUT ALSO BECAUSE WE HAVE LET OURSELVES BE CONDITIONED BY THE PICTURE THAT FAIRYTALES HAVE PAINTED OF THE BETTER KNOWN CANIDS: THUS WOLVES ARE STRONG AND BAD, FOXES ARE CUNNING, JACKALS ARE PROFITEERS AND COYOTES ARE STUPID. HOWEVER, THESE ARE JUST SENSELESS CLICHÉS. WE SHOULD OBSERVE THE WILD RELATIVES OF OUR DOMESTIC COMPANIONS AS THEY GO ABOUT THEIR DAILY LIVES WITH THE ETHOLOGIST'S EYE, IN ORDER TO REALIZE THAT THEY ARE MERELY DOGS THAT EACH OF US WOULD LIKE TO OWN.

- Two jackals assume an uncustomary erect stance as they bite each other during a fight on the Tanzanian savanna.

Wolf

496 and 497 • The wolf's size makes it the biggest and heaviest member of the large Canidae family.

498-499 • Wolves are fast and have great stamina: when hunting they can reach speeds of almost 40 mph and run for 20 minutes!

Two Gray Wolves confront each other in a forest of the Bad Mergentheim Wildlife Reserve, in Germany.

A female Gray Wolf plays with her pups in the woods in the Rocky Mountains (USA).

504-505 and 505 • Like all puppies, this young Gray Wolf in Montana (USA) loves to play, even if it is only with a feather (left), and to sleep in a warm, safe den (below).

506-507 • Several Gray Wolves skillfully and nimbly make their way through the snow of the North American Midwest.

508 and 509 • The wolf's long legs, broad paws and great stamina enable it to cover considerable distances over difficult terrain such as this in Montana (USA).

510-511 • Wolves normally travel 8-10 hours in a day, covering distances of up to 125 miles.

Dingo

Dingoes have found a favorable habitat in the grasslands of the Australian outback, where they can hunt or fight freely.

Dingoes hunt a monitor lizard in an Australian streamlet.

African Hunting Dog

* The African Hunting Dog, whose scientific name (*Lycaon pictus*) means "painted wolf" lives on the African savanna and in areas with little vegetation, where it can run exceptionally fast.

518-519 • Two young African Hunting Dogs engaged in a play fight in the grasslands of the Augrabies Falls National Park, in South Africa.

520-521 • A pack of African Hunting Dogs closes in after having sighted a prey.

Jackal

522 • These Black-Backed Jackal puppies are waiting for their mother to return to the den.

523 • Everything about the jackal – its pointed snout, well-developed ears and slender athletic frame – denotes its wild lifestyle that is a constant struggle for survival.

A Black-Backed Jackal stalks a
wood pigeon in the Etosha
National Park, in Namibia.

526-527 ● Two Black-Backed Jackals engaged in a fight in a clearing in the Etosha National Park, in Namibia.

528-529 ● The Black-Backed Jackal is distinguished by its reddish-yellow coat with longer gray hair on its back.

Coyote

- As coyotes do not form packs like wolves, they do not fight for leadership, but usually only for the possession of prey.

532 • A Coyote, a true child of the prairie, howls at the sky.

532-533 • A Coyote at rest, alert in the grass.

Fox

534 • A Red Fox takes a spectacular leap while hunting in a Colorado forest (USA).

535 • The fox's hunting method resembles that of the cat, with ambushes and sudden attacks with the front paws.

536-537 • A family of foxes hunts a skunk, attentively watched by a cub.

538 • Two Red Foxes engaged in a fight in the snowy landscape of Montana (USA).

539 • The Red Fox's face is a blaze of various hues of deep orange.

540-541 • The hare is one of the largest preys hunted by the fox, which has to subsist mainly on a diet of insects and berries.

542-543 • The fox's adaptability, and in particular its omnivorous diet, enables it to remain active and agile in snow and winter.

Arctic Species

● Winter is a hard time of year, even for the animals whose natural habitat is the northern tundra and taiga. In this season the Arctic Fox's priority is to survive, consuming its reserves of body fat and keeping itself warm, for there is very little prey to hunt.

546 • An Arctic Wolf sharpens his teeth on the antlers of a caribou, one of the most sought-after species of prey in a world where food is scarce.

547 and 548-549 • Arctic Wolves have white coats that allows them to blend in with the icy and snowy landscape.

DOGS
CATS & CO

- A little friend playfully nibbles at this German Shepherd dog. Living together is merely a matter of habit for both animals, following careful "presentation" by their owner.

INTRODUCTION Dogs, Cats & Co.

It is undeniable that certain breeds of dog have a propensity for establishing stable relations with other animals, whether wild or domestic. This is the result of selective breeding by man over thousands of years that gradually reinforced certain traits in dogs in order to obtain companions, or rather helpers, capable of interacting with the animals with which man had established relationships, usually with a practical purpose, as in the case of hunting and subsequently livestock farming. Consequently in dogs, inter-specific interactions (as ethologists call relations between animals of different species) can be so distinct,

INTRODUCTION Dogs, Cats & Co.

SPECIALIZED AND CODIFIED – EVEN IN THE OFFICIAL WORKING STANDARDS, AS IN THE SHEEPDOG BREEDS FOR EXAMPLE – THAT WE NOW HAVE EFFICIENT SHEP-HERDS CAPABLE OF LOOKING AFTER THE FLOCK EVEN IN MAN'S ABSENCE, DEFENDING IT FROM ALL KINDS OF PREDATORS OR DRIVING IT FROM THE PENS TO THE PASTURES AND VICE VERSA. THE FIRST OF THESE TASKS IS PERFORMED BY GUARDIAN SHEEPDOGS, WHICH ARE LARGE, STURDILY BUILT, STRONG AND COURAGEOUS, WHILE THE SECOND IS PERFORMED BY HERDING DOGS, WHICH ARE ALWAYS RUNNING BACK AND FORTH, READY TO GATHER UP THE FLOCK, KEEP IT TOGETHER AND DRIVE IT. HOWEVER, LEAVING ASIDE THE MANY HUNTING DOGS AND SHEEPDOGS, WHICH

INTRODUCTION Dogs, Cats & Co.

HAVE WORKING RELATIONS WITH OTHER ANIMALS AND THUS A CLEAR IDEA OF THE RAPPORT THAT THEY MUST MAINTAIN WITH THEM, THE REST OF THE CANINE WORLD OFTEN HAS VERY CONFUSED IDEAS. THIS CAN BE SEEN IN THE APPROACH OF THESE DOGS TO OTHER SPECIES, WHICH MAY BE TIMID OR EXCESSIVELY FRIENDLY, CIVIL OR AWKWARD, TOLERANT OR AGGRESSIVE, TENDER OR VIOLENT. WHY DO THESE DOGS BEHAVE LIKE THIS? THE REASON LIES IN THE FACT THAT, IN THE ABSENCE OF THE GENETIC COMPLEMENT DERIVED FROM SELECTION THAT PROPOSES THE RIGID BEHAVIORAL RULES TO BE FOLLOWED WHEN FACED WITH ANIMALS OF OTHER SPECIES, THEY HAVE DEVELOPED AND GROWN PARTIALLY INHERITING THE HABITS

INTRODUCTION Dogs, Cats & Co.

AND TASTES OF THOSE WHO BRED THEM (I.E., THE LIKES, DISLIKES OR PREJUDICES OF THESE PEOPLE TOWARDS OTHER ANIMALS) AND PARTIALLY WITH THE EXPERIENCE OF OCCASIONAL ENCOUNTERS, PERHAPS WHEN ALREADY ADULT, THAT CONTRIBUTE LITTLE TO THE FRIENDLINESS OF THEIR RELATIONS WITH OTHER SPECIES. CONSEQUENTLY, IT IS MAN – AS USUAL – WHO SHAPES THE CHARACTER OF HIS DOG AND ITS VICES AND VIRTUES. A DOG THAT IS ALLOWED TO INTERACT WITH AS MANY POSSIBLE SPECIES AS A PUPPY WILL SURPRISE YOU WITH THE INTENSITY OF THE AFFECTION THAT IT IS ABLE TO HARBOR FOR OTHER ANIMALS, DISPELLING CLICHÉS, PREJUDICES AND FALSE DEEP-ROOTED CONVICTIONS.

A moment of tension is inevitable when two young predators meet.

558-559 • This Terrier puppy has never seen a hedgehog before, otherwise he would not get so close to its spines!

560-561 • The inquisitive behavior of this young Lurcher is promising for a happy life together.

562 • If dog and cat relations prove to be impossible, in accordance with the widespread belief, then it is best for both parties if the cat has a high place to which to retreat.

563 • This pony coolly lets himself be studied by the dog. Sheepdogs have an age-old habit of interaction with other animals.

- Cats are opportunists, as this photo clearly shows: these unwitting Beagle puppies have mistaken the cat for a good-natured member of their pack.

• Although geese are undoubtedly not placid animals, they irresistibly stimulate the herding instinct.

● A warm, soft friend is always welcome. Some dogs actually have more problems relating to other dogs, especially if they are male and belong to the same breed.

This poodle and chick size each other up: curiosity is part of all young animals' makeup.

572 • Their pack-hunting instinct can sometimes make dogs aggressive towards pigs, although this is obviously not the case for this puppy.

573 • Thousands of years of interspecific interaction between dogs, livestock and man are concentrated in this face-to-face encounter between a seraphic Beagle and little pigs.

574 • Bulldogs like quiet pastimes, such as watching the pet goldfish.

575 and 576-577 • A dog's aggressiveness can be judged by his reaction towards other animals.

● Integration is complete: a puppy sleeps beside his completely trusting friend, in an almost protective pose.

This affectionate Bulldog has a low predatory instinct.

A particularly cuddly cat accepts the attentions of his canine friend, and even returns them.

This horse – which is a sensitive and sometimes unpredictable animal – is irritated by the insistence of the dog and has decided to re-establish the distance.

586-587 • Sheepdogs love the work for which they have been bred for thousands of years, whether it involves guarding the flock or herding the animals.

from 588 to 591 • Due to thousands of years of cooperation with man, dogs are far more inclined to interspecific relations than other animals and are able to relate to practically all other creatures.

LIFELONG

COMPANIONS

- A small child takes his first steps alongside his Labrador.

INTRODUCTION Lifelong Companions

IT IS IMPOSSIBLE NOT TO AGREE WITH THE ETHOLO-GIST I. EIBL-EIBESFELDT, WHO MAINTAINED THAT DOGS ARE THE ONLY MAMMALS TO HAVE REALLY LEARNED TO LIVE WITH US AND NOT SIMPLY ALONGSIDE US. IS THERE PERHAPS ANOTHER ANIMAL THAT ALSO SHARES MAN'S INTERESTS, FEELINGS AND AFFECTIONS, AS WELL AS THE SAME PHYSICAL SPACES? AND THAT SHARES THEM SO DEEPLY AS TO FEEL CALLED UPON TO LIVE AS THE EQUALS OF HUMANS IN THEIR HOMES? THERE IS AN UNWRITTEN PACT BETWEEN MAN AND DOG, WHICH WAS STIPULATED AT THE VERY MOMENT IN WHICH THE TWO DECIDE TO LIVE TOGETHER. THE DOG PERCEIVES THIS PACT AS STRONGER THAN A BLOOD BOND, LIKE AN OATH OF LOYALTY AND ABSOLUTE DEDICATION, WHICH HE WOULD NEVER BREAK AT ANY COST WITH

INTRODUCTION Lifelong Companions

CHILDREN THE PACT IS VERY SPECIAL, AND NOT JUST BE-
CAUSE PUPPIES AND CHILDREN HAVE AN INNATE ABILITY TO
RECOGNIZE EACH OTHER AS YOUNGSTERS, BUT ALSO BE-
CAUSE THEY FORM A TEAM THAT IS IMBUED WITH AN EX-
TRAORDINARY DYNAMISM. THEIR WAY OF RELATING TO
EACH OTHER REPRESENTS A TRUE EMPATHY THAT IS CAPA-
BLE OF CAPTURING THE MEANING OF NON-VERBAL SIG-
NALS, SENSING STATES OF MIND THAT ARE NOT CLEARLY
EXPRESSED AND THUS UNDERSTANDING THAT WHICH
ELUDES OTHERS WHO WATCH AND LISTEN TO US WITHOUT
EXPLORING OUR DEEPEST FEELINGS. HOWEVER, THERE'S
MORE TO IT THAN THAT. THEIR DAILY INTERACTION, WHICH
IS NEVER COMPLETELY SATISFIED, AND THE DOG'S SHORT-
ER LIFESPAN MATCHES THE CHILD'S DESIRE TO GROW UP,

Lifelong Companions
Introduction

STIMULATING A CONTINUOUS EXCHANGE OF ROLES THROUGH WHICH THE CHILD LEARNS TO DEVELOP HIS COGNITIVE ABILITIES, SOLVE PROBLEMS, DEVELOP HIS SELF-ESTEEM AND GRASP THE VERY MEANING OF LIFE. HE DOES SO BY PLAYING A SERIES OF IMPORTANT ROLES IN RAPID SUCCESSION, SUCH AS THAT OF THE AFFECTIONATE FATHER WHEN THE PUPPY IS STILL ENTIRELY DEPENDENT ON HUMAN BEINGS, THE LOYAL COMPANION WHEN THEY BOTH SHARE THE SAME UNFAILING DESIRE TO PLAY, THE DEAR SON WHEN HE FEELS THE NEED FOR THE REASSURANCE OF A STRONG AND PROTECTIVE ALLY, AND THAT OF THE RESPONSIBLE ADULT WHEN HE NEEDS TO CARE FOR HIS PREMATURELY AGED FRIEND.

* A child shows his affection for a puppy.

598-599 • A Labrador enjoys a refreshing shower.

599 • Three puppies try to escape the cleansing routines imposed by their young owners.

600 • This affectionate puppy has tired of playing and wants to be cuddled.

601 • A young Rottweiler enthusiastically fawns on his owner.

602 ● A child confronts his little Labrador face to face.

603 ● A very young cowboy poses alongside a black Labrador.

604-605 ● A Dachshund anxiously awaits his little friend's next move.

A Golden Retriever puppy leans heavily against his young friend.

A child enjoys the pleasure of a good book with a Poodle.

610 • A little girl takes her first steps supported by her dog.

611 • The Bulldog subjected to the "treatment" of these children does not seem satisfied with the work of the young "doctors."

● Golden Retrievers make excellent companions for children: they let themselves be hugged (left) and are easily tempted by candy (right).

Gluttony is a
common characteristic
of many dogs,
independent of the
breed.

616-617 ● A Golden Retriever is attracted by a smell on his owner's hand.

618-619 ● Dogs like company and adapt to unusual situations in order to be able to enjoy it.

The company of a dog is a good way for children to learn how to socialize during their early years, also in the form of friendly tussles.

622 • Children are capable of establishing immediate and spontaneous contact with animals.

623 • A small girl cradles her little dog as if it were a doll.

A very young owner learns to make friends with her Labrador, kissing him (right) and offering him a tidbit (above).

626 • A child learns to walk beneath the attentive gaze of his canine friend.

627 • A Saint Bernard enjoys the caresses of his young owner as they sit on the bank of a stream.

The harmony that is established between dogs and children sometimes creates the impression that they belong to the same family, as in the case of this dog and the two children tending to her puppies.

630 • A little girl complacently watches her dog as he lies in the grass with her.

631 • A Labrador "kisses" his owner, attracted by the ice cream on his lips.

632-633 • Play with others is fundamental for the growth of puppies and children alike.

634-635 • An absorbed child and a fairly unconcerned Bulldog play with marbles.

This little girl can enjoy carefree play with her Collie, who is a kind and protective friend.

638-639 • The liveliness of children is well suited to the playfulness of dogs.

640-641 • Four-legged friends can also be excellent study companions.

Due to the absolute
trust that dogs place in
their human friends,
caring for them is not
only enjoyable for
children, but also an
educational task that
teaches them to be
responsible.

Dogs are attentive participants in the activities of their young owners and patiently allow themselves to be enlisted in their games.

646-647 • A Basset Hound
lovingly kisses his owner.

647 • Deep reciprocal affection
can be established between a
child and a dog.

HABITS AND BEHAVIOR

The playful fight is over: the loser is pinned.

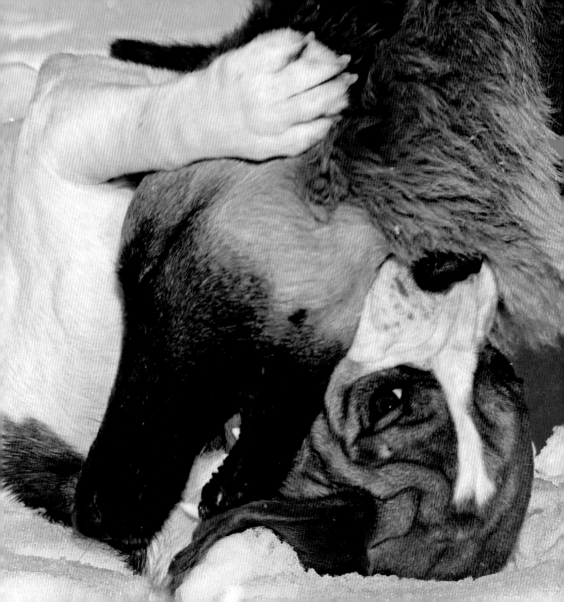

INTRODUCTION Habits and Behavior

Those of us who live with a dog can try the fascinating experiment of learning to decipher our pet's language. However, this should not be considered a mere curiosity that can be satisfied to a greater or lesser degree by the extent of our desire to understand, but essential knowledge that cannot be neglected if we truly wish to become attuned to our dog and establish a solid and happy relationship with it. Each of the two partners, dog and man, has different ways of communicating. Man relies almost exclusively on spoken language, while dogs give little importance to vocal communication, preferring body language, expressed by pose, facial expression and even movement to which they give different

INTRODUCTION Habits and Behavior

RHYTHMS, PACES AND BEARINGS. IN SHORT, DOGS SPEAK WITH THEIR WHOLE BODIES, NOT JUST BY WAGGING THEIR TAILS, AND THEIR LANGUAGE IS THE SAME WHETHER IT IS DIRECTED AT MAN OR AT MEMBERS OF THEIR OWN SPECIES. THERE IS NO OTHER WAY OF BECOMING ATTUNED TO A DOG, OR OF UNDERSTANDING WHAT DOGS SAY TO EACH OTHER, THAN BY CAPTURING THE MEANING OF THEIR GESTURES AND BEHAVIOR, AND EVEN THEIR HABITS, WHICH WE DO NOT ALWAYS SHARE. UNDERSTANDING A DOG'S NON-VERBAL LANGUAGE MEANS UNDERSTANDING THE DOG AND AVOIDING MISUNDERSTANDINGS; THIS IS THE BASIS FOR A PERSON AND A DOG TO SHARE A HAPPY LIFE TOGETHER THAT WILL BE THE SOURCE OF UNFORGETTABLE, POSITIVE EXPERIENCES. HOWEVER, IT IS NOT ENOUGH TO UNDERSTAND A DOG. IT IS NEC-

Habits and Behavior

Introduction

ESSARY THAT DOG OWNER AND DOG LEARN TO INTERACT AND RELATE TO EACH OTHER. DOGS LEARN TO DO THIS VERY SKILLFULLY BY PLAYING WITH THEIR PEERS AND WITH US; FOR THEM PLAY IS A SERIOUS ACTIVITY LIKE ALL OTHERS, AND IN-DEED THEY CONTINUE TO PLAY EVEN WHEN FULLY GROWN. IT IS THEIR WAY OF GETTING TO KNOW THE ENVIRONMENT IN WHICH THEY LIVE AND THE CREATURES THAT INHABIT IT – BOTH MAN AND OTHER ANIMALS – AND OF UNDERSTANDING WHICH ARE THE LIMITS THAT MUST NOT BE SURPASSED AND WHERE THESE LIMITS LIE. INDULGING A DOG'S HABITS, AND PLAY IN PARTICULAR, IS THUS THE BEST WAY TO REWARD IT FOR ITS FRIENDSHIP, LOYALTY AND UNWAVERING DEVOTION AND TO RECIPROCATE THE RESPECT THAT IT SHOWS US.

- Dogs are good swimmers and are usually attracted to water, like this Terrier.

- Dogs are visibly happy when they are able to vent their energy.

656, 657 and 658-659 ● A wirehaired Parson Russell Terrier, a Terrier and a Dachshund seem to fly over the ground as they run flat out.

- This lively Irish Setter displays all
the energy of the breed, both in
shaking himself dry and in
bounding through the water.

Two brave Retrievers in action in the element in which they can prove their own special skills: a Golden Retriever (above) and a Chesapeake Bay Retriever (right).

● Retrieving waterfowl is an ideal activity
for the Weimaraner, which is far too active
– and strong willed – for city life.

A Golden Retriever is overjoyed to be able to do his "job" as a water retriever.

• An energetic shake and then
it's back into the water as soon as
possible: it will be many hours
before a dog bores of this routine.

- Most dogs, whether crossbreds or purebreds like this Irish Setter, require regular exercise. If it is denied, even the mildest dog can become destructive.

Leonbergers are prudent and attentive dogs, but of course they too let themselves go in certain circumstances, such as when trying to catch a colored ball – the favorite game of many dogs.

A Pomeranian Sheepdog and a Polish Lowland Sheepdog enjoy the obstacle-free snowfields. Both are hardy dogs and well adapted to northern climes.

Running is a sheepdog's job and it is a task that it he always keen to fulfill.

These two running Collies are excited by their freedom.

● This Poodle has the breed's typically playful but not boisterous nature and is clearly delighted by his freedom.

● Young Labradors like this active and playful example remain fairly boisterous, and thus somewhat puppy-like, until the age of two years. This breed has a very gentle and friendly nature.

● Canine "sprinters": an Epagneul Bréton, above, and two three-colored
Border Collies, right.

- Terriers' behavior is said to be governed by their overwhelming desire for fun, and this playful Parson Russell Terrier does not contradict the claim.

Certain dogs are unable to resist the temptation to dig holes. This behavior is a consequence of the tasks for which they were originally bred. A sandy beach is the best place to satisfy this instinct without incurring damage.

698 and 699 ● Although a tussle is a kind of a game for dogs, it is a very compelling one, for it excites their fighting instinct.

700-701 ● The Labrador Retriever was bred as a land and water retriever for hunters over the course of a couple of centuries and is perfectly at home at the seaside.

● Running Golden Retrievers offer a spectacle of boundless energy, even though they are actually rather "self-controlled" dogs renowned for their obedience if well trained.

Dogs are playful acrobats that find it hard to resist the temptation to intercept a flying ball.

The tenaciousness of dogs can also be seen in their "tug of wars," such as this between a Collie and a Pug, who would rather let himself be dragged rather than lose his grip.

708 • Snow conceals interesting quarries for a dog with a hunting instinct.

709 • Capturing the quarry is also the motive that underlies this dynamic contest between two Borzois, the descendents of ancient sight hounds that have been trained and adapted to hunting.

● A tussle in the snow for two handsome Karelian Bear Dogs. As their name suggests, these born hunters were bred to tackle the bears of the cold Russian region.

Dogs are attracted and excited by fresh snow, in which they enjoy running and jumping.

It is quite a laborious task for a dog to scratch his back, belly in the air, but the activity almost seems to be an amusement.

• Dogs are veritable Frisbee champions, for these flying discs are far easier for them to catch than the traditional balls.

● It really does seem as though playing Frisbee is the supreme amusement for many dogs, and indeed there are veritable disc dog contests.

● Dogs will attempt comical balancing acts when the "object of their desire" is out of reach. These animals never stay still and will do everything they can to achieve their goals, like this Smooth Dachshund (above) and Cairn Terrier (right).

These crossbreds dedicate the same passionate commitment to retrieving, which is one of dogs' favorite games.

724-725 ● A Bulldog, whose gentle nature belies the terrible appearance inherited from his fierce ancestors, enjoys an impossible snack.

726-727 ● Power and nimbleness are not qualities reserved for purebred working dogs, as this handsome running crossbreed demonstrates.

INDEX

AUTHOR
Biography

VITO BUONO,
is a journalist and the author of many books about dogs and tourism. He is a reporter and correspondent for numerous newspapers and magazines. He is managing editor of the *Cinotemi* (monographs on subjects of interest to dog lovers) and *Percorsi* (tourist itineraries) series, and deputy manager of the Ciaopet and Esopo web portals dedicated to the world of animals He has organized conventions and study sessions and acted as a teacher for Bari schools and provincial government in the sphere of environmental education, with particular reference to relations between man and animals.

A

Afghan Hound, 262, 262c

African Hunting Dog, 516, 516c, 518c

Airedale Terrier, 142, 142c

Akita, 163, 163c

Alaskan Malamute, 166, 346c, 408c, 424c, 472c

American Staffordshire Terrier, 146, 146c, 436c

Arctic Fox, 544c

Arctic Wolf, 546c

Argentine Dogo, 70, 70c

Australian Cattle Dog, 412c

Australian Shepherd, 60, 60c, 420c

Australian Terrier, 140, 140c

Azawakh, 265, 265c

B

Basset Artésien-Normand, 182, 182c

Basset Hound, 11c, 176, 176c, 178c, 272c, 372c, 382c, 396c, 406c, 448c

Beagle, 184, 184c, 276c, 382c, 398c, 400c, 450c, 476c, 565c

Bearded Collie, 11c, 50, 50c

Belgian Sheepdog, 40, 40c, 439c, 461c

Bergamasco, 46, 46c

Bernese Mountain Dog, 94, 94c, 270c, 314c, 486c

Bichon Frise, 348c

Bloodhound, 180, 180c, 392c, 450c, 452c

Bobtail, see Old English Sheepdog

Bolognese, 232, 232c, 310c

Border Collie, 52, 52c, 280c, 283c, 284c, 294c, 304c,

328c, 355c, 361c, 432c, 464c, 692c

Borzoi, 256, 256c, 368c, 708c

Bouvier des Flandres, 58, 58c

Boxer, 28c, 98, 98c, 272c, 356c

Bracco Italiano, 206, 206c, 308c, 314c, 343c, 350c, 402c, 476c

Briard, 48, 48c, 384c, 406c, 674c

Brittany, 192, 192c, 692c

Bull Terrier, 135, 135c, 322c, 384c

Bulldog, 18c, 90, 90c, 92c,

235c, 366c, 380c, 456c, 468c, 470, 470c, 486c, 574c, 580c, 610c, 630c, 724c

Bullmastiff, 106, 106c, 456c, 472c

C

Cairn Terrier, 144, 144c, 720c

Cane Corso, 108, 108c, 110c

Cavalier King Charles Spaniel, 246, 246c, 376c, 426c, 434c

Chesapeake Bay Retriever, 662c

Chihuahua,

246c, 248

Chinese Crested, 242, 242c, 244c

Chinese Shar-Pei, 11c, 64, 64c, 66c, 388c, 464c

Chow Chow, 18c, 172, 172c, 278c, 340c

Cocker Spaniel, 212, 212c, 326c, 470c

Collie, 42c, 54, 54c, 637c, 686c, 707c

Coyote, 530, 530c, 532c

D

Dachshund, 152, 152c, 154c, 316c, 656c, 720c

Dalmatian, 14c,

188, 188c, 300c, 324c, 376c, 440c, 460c, 470

Dandie Dinmont Terrier, 150, 150c

Dingo, 512, 512c, 514c

Doberman Pinscher, 76, 76c, 78c

Dogue de Bordeaux, 72, 72c

E

English Cocker Spaniel, 214, 214c

English Setter, 201c

English Springer Spaniel, 225, 225c, 330c, 374c, 379c

F

Fox Terrier, 116, 116c

Fox, 534, 534c

French Bulldog, 235, 235c

G

German Pinscher, 418c

German Pointer, 195, 195c

German Shepherd Dog, 9c, 36, 36c, 39c, 332c, 550c

Golden Retriever, 216, 216c, 274c, 320c, 350c, 418c, 607c, 612c, 617c, 662c, 666c, 672c, 702c, 728c

Gordon Setter, 198, 198c, 398c

Grand Basset Griffon Vendéen, 186

Grand Griffon Vendéen, 186c

Gray Wolf, 501c, 502c, 505c

Great Dane, 100, 100c, 104c, 307 d, 380c, 390c, 417c

Greenland Dog, 160, 160c

Greyhound, 258, 258c, 470

I

Irish Setter, 201c, 202c, 660c, 670c

J

Jackal, 522, 522c, 524c, 526c

Jagdterrier, 136, 136c

K

Karelian Bear Dog, 164, 710c

Komondor, 34, 34c

L

Labrador Retriever, 11c, 216c, 218, 218c, 222c, 300c, 346c, 362c, 368c, 370c, 432c, 464c, 482c, 592c, 599c, 602c, 624c, 630c, 672c, 690c, 698c

Lakeland Terrier, 124, 124c, 328c

Leonberger, 112, 112c, 415c, 674c, 680c

Löwchen, 228, 228c

Lurcher, 558c

M

Maltese, 250, 250c

Maremma Sheepdog, 62, 62c

Mongrel, 446c

N

Neapolitan Mastiff, 88, 88c, 410c

Newfoundland, 114, 114c, 218c

Norwich Terrier, 121, 121c

O

Old English Sheepdog, 56, 56c

P

Papillon, 226, 226c

Parson Russell Terrier, 132, 132c, 310c, 316c, 336c, 361c, 362c, 423c, 436c, 446c, 656c, 694c

Pekingese, 252, 252c

Pembroke Welsh Corgi, 44, 44c, 334c

Pit Bull Terrier, 148, 148c, 344c, 394c

Pointer, 196, 196c, 366c

Polish Lowland Sheepdog, 348c, 424c, 682c

Pomeranian Sheepdog, 674c, 682c

Pomeranian, 174

Poodle, 32c, 238, 238c, 570c, 688c

Pug, 236, 236c, 707c

R

Red Fox, 534c, 538c, 540c

Rottweiler, 74, 74c, 266c, 336c, 600c

Rough Collie, 672c

S

Saint Bernard, 84, 84c, 87c, 302c, 318c, 338c, 626c

Samoyed, 158, 158c, 338c

Schnauzer, 80, 80c, 83c, 446c

Scottish Terrier, 118, 118c

Sheltie, see Shetland Sheepdog

Shetland Sheepdog, 42, 42c

Shih Tzu, 230, 430c

Siberian Husky, 168, 168c, 374c, 481c, 482c

Skye Terrier, 126, 126c

W

Weimaraner, 209, 209c, 210c, 665c

Welsh Terrier, 122, 122c

West Highland White Terrier, 118, 118c, 440c

Wirehaired Pointing Griffon, 204, 320c

Wolf, 496, 496c, 508c

Y

Yorkshire Terrier, 128, 128c, 130, 334c

PHOTO CREDITS

PHOTO CREDITS

Martin Harvey/ Corbis/Contrasto: page 513

Martin Harvey/NHPA: page 703

Elizabeth Hathon/Corbis/ Contrasto: pages 628-629

Walter Hodges/Corbis/ Contrasto: pages 612, 613

Ernie Janes: pages 52, 53, 98, 189

Ernie Janes/NHPA: page 272

Daniel J.Cox: pages 491, 496, 498-499, 502, 503, 504-505, 505, 506-507, 508

Daniel J.Cox/Corbis/Contrasto: page 509

Nigel J Dennis/NHPA: pages 520-521

Ronnie Kaufman/Corbis/ Contrastro: page 601

Layne Kennedy/Corbis/ Contrasto: page 562

Ron Kimball/Ron Kimball Stock: pages 64, 346, 418, 482, 580-581, 662, 688-689, 694-695, 702, 719, 726-727

T. Kitchin & V. Hurst/NHPA: page 544

Jean Michel Labat/Ardea: pages 2-3, 54, 168, 684-685

Renee Lynn/Corbis/Contrasto: pages 185, 458-459, 694

Gerard Lacz/NHPA: page 551

Gerard Lacz/PandaPhoto: pages 50, 210

Yves Lanceau/NHPA: page 715

Frans Lanting/Corbis/ Contrasto: page 523

L. Lenz/Blickwinkel: pages 584, 584-585

Luckylook/DanitaDelimont.co m: page 575

Renee Lynn/Corbis/Contrasto: pages 185, 458-459, 694

LWA-Dann Tardif/Corbis/ Contrasto: pages 442, 486, 574, 597, 611, 634-635

Don Mason/Corbis/Contrasto: page 446

Joe McDonald/ Corbis/Contrasto: pages 510-511

Roy Morsch/Corbis/Contrasto: page 622

Ulrich Neddens/Archiv Boiselle: pages 24-25, 38-39,55, 78, 79, 96-97, 112, 113, 154-155, 202-203, 294, 294-295, 300, 304-305; 414-415, 415, 419, 450, 649, 656, 657, 660, 660-661, 668, 668-669, 670, 671, 672, 673, 674, 674-675, 678-679, 680, 681, 682, 683, 685, 686-687, 692, 693, 696, 704, 705, 706-707, 708

James Noble/Corbis/Contrasto: pages 220-221

Charles O'Rear/ Corbis/Contrasto: pages 724-725

Gabe Palmer/Corbis/Contrasto: page 623

• A Golden Retriever stares inquisitively at the lens, attentive to what is going on around him. Many dogs are very sensitive to their environments and sometimes seem to have a "sixth sense" – particularly in respect to ill-intentioned humans – which is perhaps associated with smell.